Inventions

A thousand years of bright ideas and the science that inspired them

By Anne Rooney

Ticktock

Contents

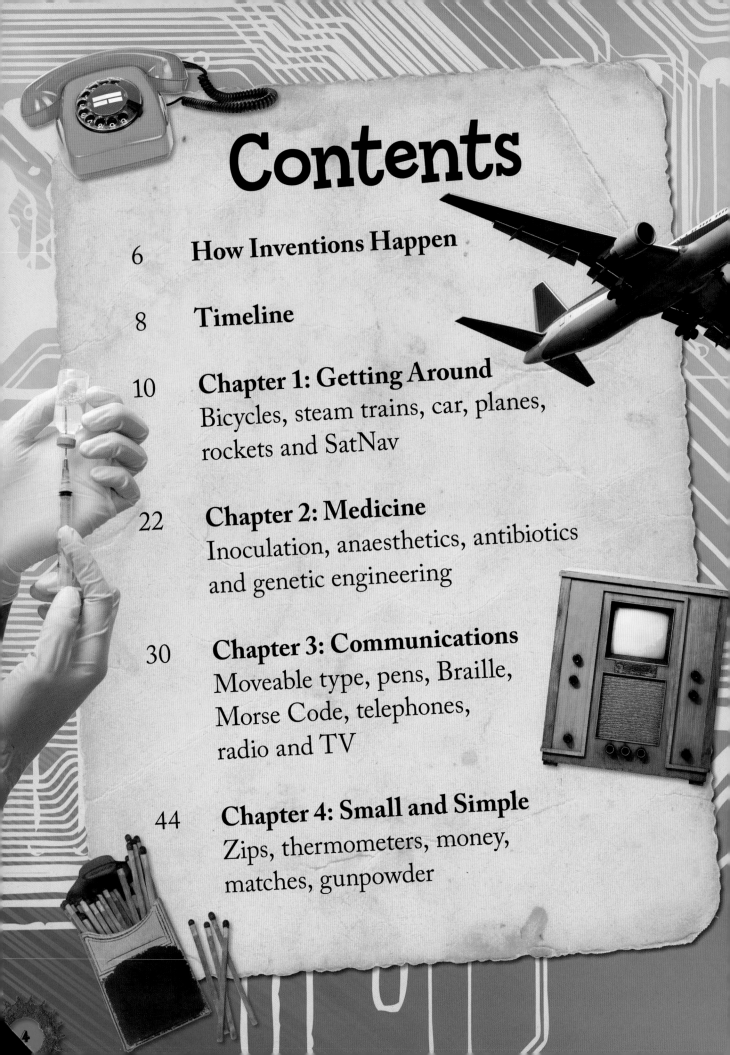

6   **How Inventions Happen**

8   **Timeline**

10   **Chapter 1: Getting Around**
Bicycles, steam trains, car, planes, rockets and SatNav

22   **Chapter 2: Medicine**
Inoculation, anaesthetics, antibiotics and genetic engineering

30   **Chapter 3: Communications**
Moveable type, pens, Braille, Morse Code, telephones, radio and TV

44   **Chapter 4: Small and Simple**
Zips, thermometers, money, matches, gunpowder

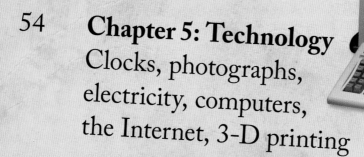

54   **Chapter 5: Technology**
Clocks, photographs,
electricity, computers,
the Internet, 3-D printing

66   **Chapter 6: Sight and Sound**
Glasses, microscopes,
telescopes, phonographs

74   **Chapter 7: Materials**
Yarn, cotton, modern materials

80   **Chapter 8: At Home**
Toilets, canned food, refrigeration,
sewing machines, electric light

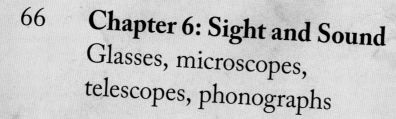

90:   **What's Left to Invent?**

92   **Glossary**

94   **Index**

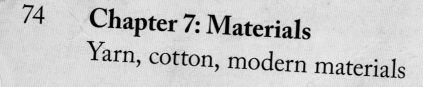

How inventions happen

People have been inventing things for thousands of years. To start with, they made simple tools like **spears** and **knives**. As time passed, all the obvious things were invented. But gradually people invented more and more things to make life easier, or help them have fun.

I'm Tockington and I'll be your guide to a thousand years of great inventions!

Some inventions, like the computer, are very complicated and combine the work of lots of people over a long time – sometimes hundreds of years.

Others are very simple, but still important. Barbed wire, invented in France in 1860, made the vast cattle ranches of America possible.

There's a famous saying, that "necessity is the mother of invention". It means we invent things when we really need them. But not all inventions are needed. The **aeroplane** came about because people longed to fly. Other things are invented entirely by accident.

Many of the most important inventions are components that make other things possible. The **steam engine**, the **electric motor**, the **transistor**, the **silicon chip** and the **integrated circuit board** have led to many more exciting inventions.

Sometimes, a scientific discovery leads to new ideas. Finding that waves of **electromagnetic radiation** travel through air and space led to lots of inventions, including **radio** and **mobile phones**, as people experimented ` and thought creatively.

Timeline

Some of the most important inventions have been around for thousands of years. They include the wheel, the pulley, the spear, pottery, rope, irrigation systems (for watering crops) and the plough.

Gunpowder
(China, about 1000)

Printing
(Bi Sheng, China, 1045)

Clockwork
(Europe, about 1300)

Not all inventions are popular. In the early 1800s, a group of factory workers known as the **Luddites** smashed automated weaving machinery because it threatened to take over their jobs in the textile industry.

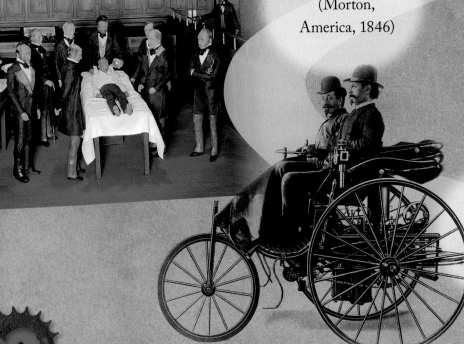

Telegraph
(Morse, America, 1838)

Anaesthetic
(Morton, America, 1846)

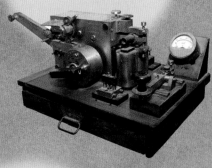

Car
(Benz, Germany, 1886)

Printed books
(Gutenberg, 1439,
Germany)

Microscope
(Netherlands,
about 1600)

Many inventions extend lives, make our daily routine easier, or free people from dull work to do more interesting jobs. But this also means that things can't be uninvented, even if they turn out to be bad for us, like cigarettes and machine guns.

Vaccination
(Jenner, England,
1796)

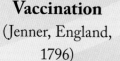

Antibiotics
(Fleming,
England, 1928)

World Wide Web
(Berners Lee, 1991,
Switzerland)

CHAPTER 1: GETTING AROUND

We've always been able to travel by walking, or riding animals. But sometimes we want to go faster. To get going at any speed, we've needed machines.

Where are you going?

The earliest travellers used the sun by day and the stars by night to **navigate**. But that only works if it's not cloudy and you know what to look for.

A better way is to use a **compass**. The first compasses for navigation were made in China around 1040.

They used a steel needle, magnetized using the naturally magnetic mineral called lodestone, fixed to a bamboo pin. Magnetized iron or steel naturally lines up with the Earth's magnetic field, so the needle turned on the pin until it was pointing north/south.

The Earth's magnetic field extends Earth's core into space.

Before

Before compasses, Chinese craftsmen made a ladle (a type of spoon) from magnetic iron ore. Placed on a smooth surface, it swivelled so that the handle pointed south. It was used for mystic rituals such as choosing a lucky burial site.

The first person known to have a navigational compass was Zheng He, a Chinese sea-explorer from Yunnan province, in China. He used it between 1405 and 1433.

The wheel was the first transport invention, about 5,000 years ago. It's easy to make one from a slice of tree!

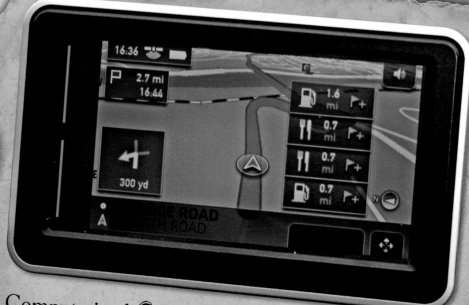

Computerized **SatNav** – Satellite Navigation – is easier to use than a compass. Signals beamed from **satellites** in space tell the SatNav device exactly where it is. The device's inbuilt computer then uses stored maps to work out a route The first SatNav system was made in Japan, in 1990.

Get pedalling!

A bicycle is a wonderful thing – it means you can use your own muscle power, with no fuel, to move faster and further than you could by walking.

The first bicycles had wooden wheels and iron tyres, so they were very bumpy and uncomfortable to ride. They were often called bone-shakers! Their real name was the **velocipede**, and they were manufactured by the French Michaux company from 1867 to 1869. Turning the pedals turned the front wheel directly.

Before

Stephan Farffler was a disabled watchmaker from Nuremberg, now in Germany. In 1655 he made himself a tricycle wheelchair that he drove by turning a handle.

Made possible by... better metals

Developments in metallurgy (the science of metals) meant it was possible to make small, strong parts and suitable chains for the first time.

By 1870 there were high-wheel bicycles, like the **Penny-Farthing**, which were more comfortable to ride. The huge front wheel meant the bicycle went further with every turn of the pedals. Unfortunately it also made the bicycle much more dangerous.

It was a long way to the ground if you fell off!

The modern **"safety" bicycle** was invented in the UK by Thomas Humber in 1868. It was safe because both wheels were the same size, the rider's feet could reach the ground so it was easier to stop, and the pedals turned the back wheel, keeping the feet away from the front wheel. Humber's biggest brainwave was to add a chain to the bone-shaker, connecting the pedals to the back wheel.

Bicycling soon became massively popular around the world.

On the right track

A train needs a railway and trucks pulled by a powered engine. The two were brought together by Richard Trevithick to make the first workable steam train, the *Puffing Devil*, in England in 1804.

The first passenger trains carried just a few people in open trucks. The steam and smoke from the engine made it uncomfortable, and people were worried that going as fast as 25kph would be harmful. But the train was too useful to abandon. In the 1800s, **railroads** became the first big business in America, enabling people and tools to reach huge areas of land too hard to reach otherwise.

Made possible by... the piston steam-engine

Thomas Newcomen invented the steam engine in England around 1710. It was first used for pumping water. James Watt improved the steam engine enough to drive a wheel, but his first engines were too large and heavy to use in a vehicle. Watt's company eventually made a working **locomotive** in 1794.

Before trains, everything had to be moved by muscle power!

Burning coal heats water, making steam. The pressure of the steam moves a piston in a cylinder. The **piston** has a rod attached to a crank, which turns the wheels.

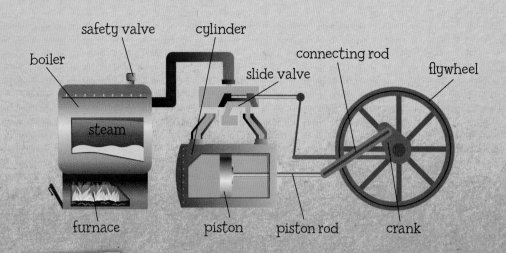

boiler · safety valve · cylinder · connecting rod · flywheel · slide valve · steam · furnace · piston · piston rod · crank

Before

Tracks made of grooves cut into rock were used for hauling loads in Greece 2,600 years ago. In the 1550s, men or horses pulled chains of trucks loaded with coal through coalmines in Germany. They used a slightly more sophisticated system, where a pin under the trucks fitted into a groove between wooden tracks.

After

After steam, engines were powered by **diesel** and then electricity. Super-fast Maglev trains float above the track by means of a system of magnets.

Many countries use Maglev trains, which go very fast because there is no **friction between the rails and the train.**

Going by car

The first cars looked nothing like the ones you see today – they were more like horse-drawn carriage without horses!

That nifty vehicle could reach 16 kph.

The first **car** was made by Karl Benz in Germany in 1886. It would have been a very uncomfortable ride. The people sitting on the hard seat would have felt every bump the steel-rimmed wheels went over (and there were lots of bumps in the roads in those days). The car had no roof, doors or windscreen to keep the weather out.

Early improvements included pneumatic (air-filled) tyres for a cushioned ride, a **starter motor** – and a roof.

Bertha's big adventure

The first long-distance car journey was made by Karl's wife, Bertha, in 1888. Without telling Karl, she set out with their two sons to drive 106 km to visit her mother. On arrival at her mother's house, Bertha sent her husband a telegram. Bertha invented brake linings, getting a shoe-maker to nail leather to the **brake** blocks. Finding the car couldn't climb hills, she suggested Benz add a second gear.

The **Model T Ford** was first made by Henry Ford's Motor Company in 1908. Ford wanted to bring cars to the American public. His cars were affordable because they were made in a factory on a production line rather than being hand-crafted.

Made possible by ...
the internal combustion engine

The internal combustion engine, designed in 1807, works by setting fire to fuel in an enclosed space. The force of the fuel exploding pushes a piston connected by a rod to a motor. This happens again and again, very quickly.

The Model T was affordable for ordinary middle-class families.

Modern cars work on the same basic principle as the original versions - but they go a lot faster!

Up, up and away

The first powered flight in a fixed-wing aircraft was achieved by the American brothers Orville and Wilbur Wright in 1903 – but only just!

The Wright brothers practised by making lots of other machines and plenty of gliders which they flew successfully. Their first powered **"flying machine"** succeeded where others failed because they put effort into controlling the plane in all directions – backwards and forwards, up and down, and rolling side to side. Their plane was made from spruce wood and muslin, a very light, thin fabric. On its first successful flight, Orville flew 37 m in 12 seconds (a speed of 10.9 kph) at a height of 10 m above the ground.

From

1914: Planes used in combat in World War I

1939: First jet plane, Heinkel He 178, tested in Germany

1947: First manned supersonic flight (faster than the speed of sound)

1952: First jet airliner, de Havilland Comet

2005: First flight by the world's largest passenger plane, the Airbus A380. It can carry 853 passengers.

Before

In 1777, Joseph Montgolfier saw his laundry billowing as it dried by the fire. He sent a letter to his brother, saying: "Get in a supply of **taffeta** and of **cordage**, quickly, and you will see one of the most astonishing sights in the world." They worked hard, and in 1783, they made a hot-air balloon which carried a sheep, a rooster and a duck on a test flight. It flew 3 km in 8 minutes and reached a height of about 460 m. The next flight carried human passengers.

An early hot-air balloon.

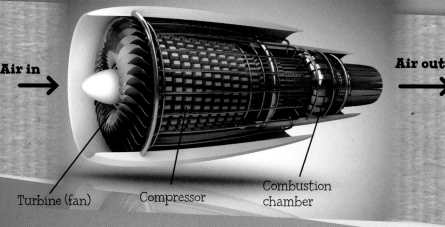

Air in →

Air out →

Turbine (fan) Compressor Combustion chamber

Jet Engine

Air is sucked in by a fan at the front, compressed and mixed with fuel. The mixture burns and expands, pushing out of the back and spinning the fan, which pulls in more air.

I wonder if I could be fitted with a jet engine?

Blasted into space

The first multi-stage **rockets** were launched in China around 700 years ago. The "fire-dragon issuing from the water" was a weapon powered by gunpowder, described in the 1300s. A single rocket shaped liked a dragon whizzed into the sky, and then several smaller rockets fired from the dragon's mouth.

The American inventor Robert Goddard first fired a rocket that used **liquid fuel** (liquid oxygen and petrol) in 1926. His most successful rocket launch reached a height of 2.6 km and flew at 885 kph. No one took his rocket designs very seriously until after his death.

In Germany, Wernher von Braun was keen to design rockets for **space exploration**. He launched his first two A4 rockets in 1934, and they rose 2.2 and 3.5 km into the air. But when World War II broke out, his rockets were renamed V2 and used as bombs.

Americans test a V2 rocket after World War II.

After the war, von Braun went to the USA where he worked on the **NASA space programme**. His rocket dreams eventually came true when the first rockets were launched into space in the 1950s. The first rocket to land on the moon was Luna 2 in 1959.

A rocket works in the same way as a jet engine: as a rocket burns fuel, the exhaust gases rush out of the rocket's back end, forcing it forwards. As there's no air in space, a space rocket needs to carry its own supply of air to burn its fuel.

Some rockets carry robots into space, or even to explore other planets. I want to go!

CHAPTER 2: MEDICINE

Long ago, doctors could do little to help most people who were sick or injured. You're lucky to live in an age when there have been lots of advances in medicine.

Just a little jab

Going for a jab is probably not your favourite thing to do, but it could save your life. **Vaccination** can now protect us from diseases that have killed millions of people in the past.

Smallpox is a deadly disease that causes a rash of spots filled with pus. Around 1,000 AD, Chinese doctors started taking pus from the spots and drying it, then giving it to healthy people, either puffed into their noses or put into scratches on their skin. The process was called **"variolation"**. People who had been variolated rarely caught smallpox.

Some robots even carry out surgery now!

An early demonstration of vaccination.

How it works

When the body meets a new germ, it creates antibodies to fight it. The body then remembers how to make the antibodies in case they're needed later. Inoculation uses a tiny, safe dose of the germ so that your body works out how to make antibodies. If you encounter the real disease later, your body is ready to make antibodies.

A statue of Jenner vaccinating a child.

Variolation (**inoculation**) came to Europe in 1718. It was better than nothing, but there was a small risk of variolation itself causing infection. English doctor Edward Jenner found a better way in 1796. He saw that milkmaids with cowpox (which is not dangerous) never caught smallpox. He used pus from cowpox spots to make a much safer **vaccine**. Vaccination was so successful that smallpox was wiped out by 1980.

Anaesthetics

Imagine having your teeth pulled out or your leg cut off without an anaesthetic to stop it hurting. It wouldn't be good, would it? But millions of people before us have had to put up with that. We've had **anaesthetics** – medicines that stop us feeling pain – for fewer than 200 years.

In the past, alcohol or medicine made from **opium** (medicine made from poppies) helped reduce pain, but not by much. Then in 1846, American dentist

William Morton used the chemical **ether** to put a patient to sleep while he cut a tumour from the man's neck. Ether is a liquid that boils at just above room temperature, so it's easy to breathe in the fumes, particularly if it is boiled in a bowl and the fumes funnelled towards the patient's face through a tube.

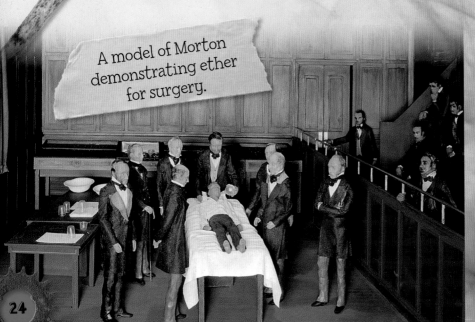

A model of Morton demonstrating ether for surgery.

Luckily, I can't feel anything if I need to be fixed.

Gone - and forgotten

It's reported that the Chinese surgeon Hua Tuo used a general anaesthetic (one that puts people completely to sleep) in the second century, but the recipe has not survived. It may be that for a while people in China had painless operations.

Before anaesthetics, surgeons could only carry out very short operations such as cutting off limbs. Anything else took too long – the patients' pain made them struggle, and the shock often killed them. With anaesthetics, surgeons could begin to operate inside the body. **General anaesthetics** make the patient unconscious so that they can't feel anything and they can't move. **Local anaesthetics** make just one part of the body numb. They are injected, or are rubbed onto the body as a cream. The first local anaesthetic was used in 1884 for eye operations.

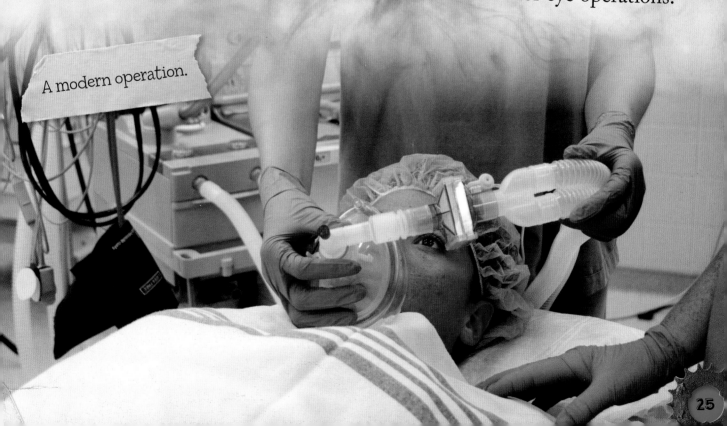

A modern operation.

Germ-killers

Cutting open the body for an operation makes it very easy for germs to get in and cause deadly infections. By making operations easier, anaesthetics made problems with infections worse.

Luckily, in the 1860s, the British surgeon Joseph Lister found that if he operated on patients under a spray of carbolic acid, the acid mist killed germs and his patients did not develop infections. He had invented **antisepsis** – killing germs in the environment and on the body. Even complicated operations became much safer. Today, surgical instruments are **sterilized** with heat and chemicals, surgeons wear sterile clothes, and hospitals are cleaned with antiseptics.

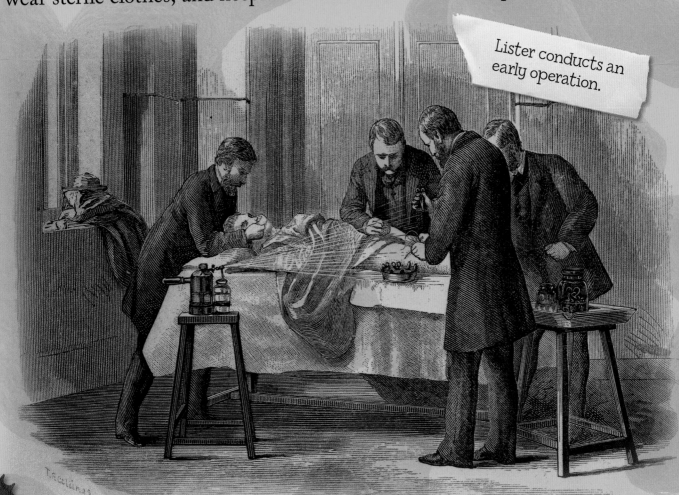

Lister conducts an early operation.

While antiseptics kill germs before they get a chance to cause infection, **antibiotics** kill germs inside the body after an infection has taken hold. The Scottish biologist **Alexander Fleming** discovered the first antibiotic in 1928. He was growing **bacteria** on dishes of special jelly, and piled up his used dishes before going on holiday – but he didn't wash them up. When he came back, he saw that some of the bacteria had died where mould had grown on the plates. He found the penicillium mould had produced a chemical which killed the bacteria.

The first antibiotic, called **penicillin**, was developed for medical use by Ernst Chain and Howard Florey in 1941. Antibiotics have saved millions of lives.

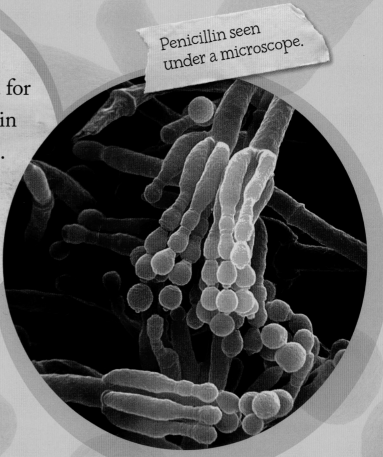

Penicillin seen under a microscope.

Surgical robots don't have to wash their hands – but they are kept sterile.

Golden rice and glowing mice

For thousands of years, farmers have changed animals' **genes** by choosing which ones to let breed together. But now scientists have done the same by altering the **DNA** (genetic material) in cells. This is called genetic engineering.

The German biologist Rudolf Jaenisch was the first person to mix **DNA** from different species in 1974. He added DNA from a **virus** to a mouse **embryo** and found it fused with the mouse DNA and appeared in all the cells of the adult mouse.

Similar methods have been used to make **genetically modified (GM) foods**. Some of these foods can stay fresh longer before going bad, some foods resist disease or bugs while they're growing, and some foods have more **nutrients** than the non-modified versions. Golden rice has genes from daffodils and contains more vitamin A than unmodified rice.

Scientists often add a "glow-in-the-dark" gene, taken from a jellyfish, to test techniques for making genetic changes. There have been glow-in-the dark mice, rabbits, cats and cockroaches.

A scientist looks at GM plants in a lab.

If your glow-in-the-dark pet mouse escaped, it would be easy to spot!

One current genetic engineering project aims to breed mammals (such as cows and sheep) that will produce medicines in their milk, making it easy to supply low-cost treatments in countries without large **pharmaceutical** factories.

29

CHAPTER 3: COMMUNICATIONS

We communicate by writing and talking. We may speak just to people nearby, or to millions of others, or to people on the other side of the world. Inventions in communications technology have made that possible.

Words on the page

Before computers, all books were made using **moveable type** – tiny blocks, each with one letter, which could be rearranged to make words, sentences, and pages of text. And before *that*, all books were handwritten, which took a very long time.

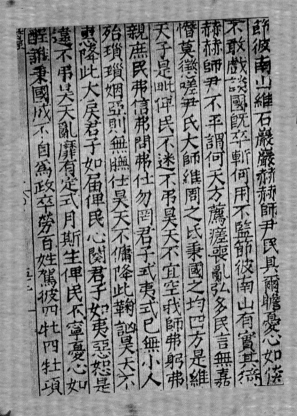

The first moveable type was developed in China in 1045 by **Bi Sheng**. He used **porcelain type**, which was fragile. In the early 1300s, **Wang Zhen** developed **wooden type**, which was stronger. As printers didn't have to be as careful with it, they could work more quickly.

Chinese printers didn't make books: they printed onto long strips of paper or fabric that could be rolled up. They were called **scrolls**.

Pʒelũ Alcẽhanũ

In around 1439, the German blacksmith Johannes Gutenberg also invented moveable type. He went further, though, by making a **printing press**. The type – one metal block for each letter – was arranged in a frame and covered with ink. Then Gutenberg laid paper over the block. Another block of wood was put on to that, which was pressed down by winding a large screw. The ink was transferred to the paper and, hey presto, a page of words!

Gutenberg printed **books**, not scrolls. They were easier to use, as you could skip straight to any page. The printing press soon flooded Europe with books, and far more people learned to read.

Moveable type might be the most important invention of the last 1,000 years.

Right - get writing!

From early times, people wrote by using a stick or feather. It was a slow process because you had to dip your pen into ink every few words. Even after the invention of printing, people wanted ways of writing faster.

In 973, the caliph (leader) of Maghreb (part of North Africa) demanded a pen that would not stain his hands. Someone made one for him. It held ink inside it and could be used upside-down, but we don't know anything else about it.

In Germany in 1636 an early **fountain pen** was made using one quill (the 'stalk' of a feather) inside another, the outer one filled with ink and sealed with cork. In 1663, Samuel Pepys had a metal pen that could "carry ink". Modern fountain pens appeared in the 1800s, when rubber became available to hold a supply of ink, called the ink bladder.

A French pen advert from the 1910s.

Porte Plume "Ideal"
Waterman
l'Arme de la pa

In 1868, Christopher Sholes, Carlos Glidden, and Samuel Soule made the first proper **typewriter** in the USA. It used the QWERTY layout that still appears on computer keyboards.

A 20th-century typewriter.

Filling a fountain pen was a chore. The very first **ballpoint pen** was invented in 1888, but it used ordinary runny ink. The Hungarian **Laslo Biro** invented the first ballpoint to use thick ink that didn't smudge, in 1938. He called it... yes the Biro. Biro **patented** his pen in the UK.

A patent registers ownership of a design. Copycats can't pinch it!

Words without speaking

Most of us communicate by speaking and reading.
But people who can't see or hear need different methods.

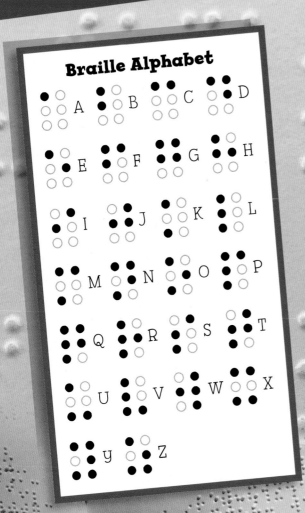

Braille Alphabet

A B C D
E F G H
I J K L
M N O P
Q R S T
U V W X
Y Z

Braille is a written code of raised dots used by people who can't see to read. Louis Braille developed the code in 1824 after he was blinded in an accident at only 15 years old. Each letter of the alphabet is represented by an arrangement of up to six raised dots.
In 1829, Braille extended his system to cover musical notation. Before that, blind people had to read raised text with normal letters, which was very difficult to do.

American Sign Language is closer to French Sign Language than to British! It's based on a French sign language from the 1750s

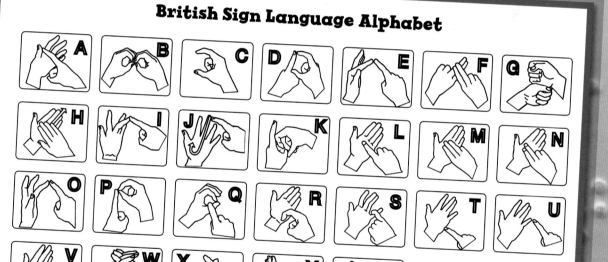

British Sign Language Alphabet

People who can't hear often use a **sign language** made up of finger-spellings and hand gestures that stand for whole words. There are different sign languages in different countries. Forms of sign language were used in deaf communities in Britain from around 1570. In 1760, Thomas Braidwood constructed a consistent code and taught it in the first school for deaf pupils, in Edinburgh. This formed the basis of British Sign Language.

Dots and dashes

In the past, the only way you could communicate with someone who had gone away was by letter – a letter that might take weeks to reach them if they were overseas.

Morse Code was the first method of fast long-distance communication, developed by Samuel Morse in 1838. It worked by sending tiny pulses of electricity along a wire, then using the electricity to make a magnet move a marker at the other end. The marker made dots and dashes on paper, forming a code. To send a message, the telegraph operator tapped on a "key" that briefly made an electrical contact and sent a pulse. Later, skilled telegraph operators listened to the signals and wrote a copy of the message on to a piece of paper, translating the code into letters that anyone could read.

Samuel Morse.

An earlier attempt at long-distance communication made in Scotland in 1753 used a separate wire for each letter of the alphabet!

Made possible by...
the electromagnet

In 1820, the Danish scientist **Hans Christian Ørsted** discovered that electric current creates a magnetic field. Four years later, **William Sturgeon** developed a powerful electromagnet. By running an electric current through copper wire wrapped around a 200-gram piece of iron he could lift a lump of iron weighing 4kg. The electric current magnetizes the piece of metal in the middle. It only acts as a magnet while the current is turned on.

Morse Code

A	·—	P	·——·
B	—···	Q	——·—
C	—·—·	R	·—·
D	—··	S	···
E	·	T	—
F	··—·	U	··—
G	——·	V	···—
H	····	W	·——
I	··	X	—··—
J	·———	Y	—·——
K	—·—	Z	——··
L	·—··	Full stop	·—·—·—
M	——	Comma	——··——
N	—·	Message	
O	———	Ends	·—·—·

Three people worked on developing **telegraphy** at the same time. Morse was the first to succeed. He opened the first working telegraph line in 1844 in the USA, sending the message "What hath God wrought?"

A word in your ear

Today's smart phones have come a long way from the very first telephones! The first patent for a phone was filed by Alexander Graham Bell in America in 1876, though there have been arguments over whether he came up with the technology first.

The first **telephones** had to have a wire directly connecting any two phones that people wanted to make calls between. That wasn't a lot of use – it meant you could only call someone else if their phone was directly wired to yours.

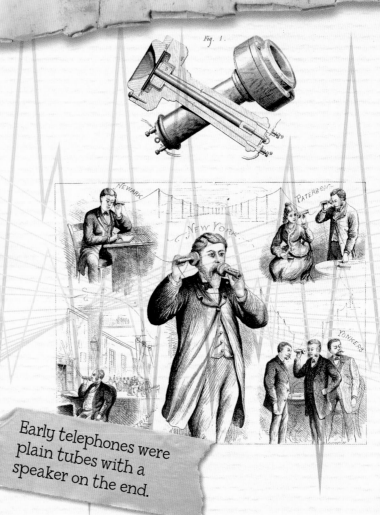

Early telephones were plain tubes with a speaker on the end.

Luckily, just after Bell invented the telephone, the Hungarian engineer **Tivadar Puskás** developed a switch which made it possible to build a **telephone exchange**. In the early days, an operator had to connect every call, putting a plug into the right socket to connect one person's phone to the other.

An early telephone exchange.

Telephone numbers were very short when there were very few phones – often just three numbers long.

In the late 19th and early 20th centuries, some rural farming communities in the USA used the barbed wire fences around their fields to carry telephone signals! Soon, telephone cables were strung across the land, held up by poles or buried underground.

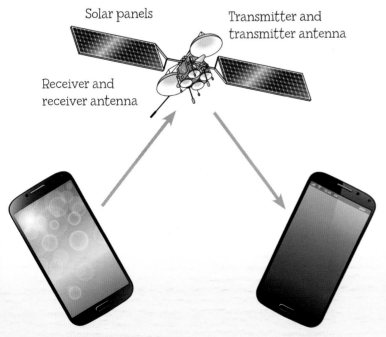

Solar panels

Transmitter and transmitter antenna

Receiver and receiver antenna

Mobile phones don't use wires at all. They use radio signals that are bounced off satellites to travel round the world at the speed of light.

Over the airwaves

Heinrich Hertz first demonstrated radio in Germany in 1887, but he thought it was of little practical use.

Radio codes information onto waves of electromagnetic radiation as a way of transmitting messages over long distances. It starts with a radio transmitter, which turns information such as sound, pictures or computer data into coded radio waves. These are beamed through the air, or space. At the other end, a receiver decodes the signal and turns it back into sound, pictures or data.

Made possible by... electromagnetic radiation

In 1865, James Clerk Maxwell made one of the most important scientific discoveries since Newton explained gravity. He worked out that electromagnetic radiation travels through air (or space) as waves. We experience waves of different **wavelength** as light, radio, X-rays, microwaves and so on. All travel at the speed of light. Electromagnetic radiation gives us radio, television, mobile phone signals, radar and other useful technologies.

A mobile radio station used by Marconi (below) and a modern transmitter (opposite).

Guiglielmo Marconi filed a patent for a radio in 1897. At first, radio was used like telegraphy, to send messages in Morse code. Its first main use was for ships to communicate with the shore and with each other.

Marconi's early equipment was clunky and fragile.

From then to now

1866: American dentist Mahlon Loomis demonstrated "wireless telegraphy", sending a signal between two meters connected to kites – the first-ever wireless communication

1899: Guiglielmo Marconi sent the first radio signal across the English Channel

1902: Marconi made the first wireless transatlantic communication – the letter "S"

1912: While the *Titanic* was sinking, its radio operators used the ship's radio to send the new Morse code signal SOS to call for help. Afterwards, most large ships carried radios.

1915: The first sound-only radio transmission

1916: The first regular radio broadcasts – the weather forecast, in Morse code, for Wisconsin, USA

1919: First successful transmission of human speech

1920: Regular broadcasts for entertainment begin, in Argentina

1954: First pocket **transistor** radio

1993: First Internet radio show; Internet radio needs no radio transmitter.

I have a built-in radio receiver!

41

From radio, it's a small step to television. If you can send sound through the air, why not pictures?

The Scottish engineer **John Logie Baird** first demonstrated **television** in the London shop Selfridge's, in 1926. All it showed was moving silhouette (outline) images – but it was a start. Later the same year, Kenjiro Takayanagi showed the first **cathode ray tube** television in Japan.

The earliest western televisions were **electromechanical**, using spinning discs with holes in to generate and display the pictures. From 1934, Telefunken in Germany made commercial televisions using cathode ray tubes.

In the late 1920s, Baird also demonstrated versions of colour television and even 3D-television and the infra-red television that is now used for CCTV cameras. It was many years before these would be generally available.

A German cathode ray tube television from 1935.

There's no point having a television with no broadcasts to watch. The world's first electronic television service started in Berlin in 1935, but the real start of television is generally considered to be in 1936 when the **BBC** began regular broadcasts.

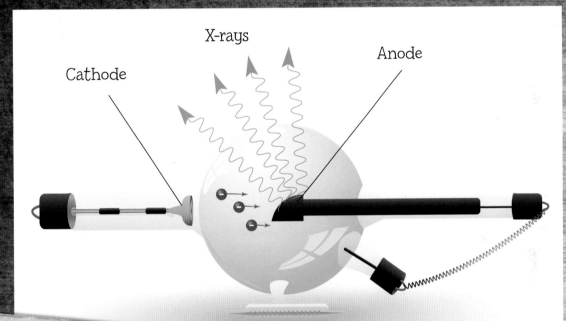

Cathode

X-rays

Anode

Made possible by...
the cathode ray tube

A cathode ray tube produces a stream of **electrons** which pass through a **vacuum** and strike a phosphorus-coated screen, making it glow. The beam of electrons passes very quickly across the screen in lines, striking spots on the screen to make a picture. It's so fast that we see the stream of pictures as a moving image.

Today's technology means there's no need for a huge box behind the screen!

Modern flat-screen TVs use LED (light-emitting diode) technology.

Not all inventions are large and dramatic. Some are really small and simple, but they make a world of difference to our lives. Imagine life without matches or money!

Fast fastenings

The first fastenings were laces and ribbons. Then came buttons and hooks. And now we have some zappier options.

There's **zips** on your clothes and possibly on your bag. The zip was invented by Elias Howe in 1851. He patented the design, but made his fortune from inventing sewing machines (see page 86) and never got around to perfecting and manufacturing zips.

Instead, a Swedish-American engineer called Gideon Sundback started selling zips in 1913. After wrestling with problems such as the zip pulling apart, he finalized the design of the interlocking teeth and soon his factory was producing 100 metres of metal zips each day.

Burrs on a plant.

If De Mestral had owned a short-haired dog, there'd be no Velcro!

One day in 1941, the electrical engineer George de Mestral took his dog out in the Swiss Alps. Afterwards, he had to pick burrs from his dog's coat. Examining some burrs under his microscope, he found they had tiny hooks, and these had snagged the dog's fur. De Mestral decided that he could make a good fastener using the same idea. It was difficult to get right, and it didn't sell at first, but these days we know this product as **Velcro**. When NASA started to use Velcro fastenings for spacesuits and other space equipment, its popularity soared.

Modern velcro.

Hot and cold

We use thermometers to measure temperature – for checking the weather, cooking our food, finding out whether sick people have a fever, and lots of other uses.

The first **thermometer** with a scale was invented in England by Robert Fludd in 1638. It was a glass tube, open at one end. The open end was placed in a bowl of water and the other (closed) end had air in. As the temperature rose, the air in the tube expanded and pushed the water down the tube and back into the bowl. Since the air pressure outside the tube also affected the level of water inside the tube, it was a combined thermometer and **barometer**.

Experimenting with an early thermometer.

In 1654, the Italian Grand Duke **Ferdinando II de' Medici** designed a closed thermometer filled with alcohol. It looked like a modern glass thermometer, as it had a bulb-shape at the bottom, and a glass shaft, and was sealed at both ends. As the thermometer was closed, the outside air pressure didn't affect the thermometer.

At first, each thermometer-maker chose their own scale. Then in 1724 Daniel Gabriel **Fahrenheit** invented a thermometer which contained mercury (a liquid metal) and proposed a measurement scale that could become a standard. In 1742 **Anders Celsius** devised a scale with zero as the boiling point of water and 100 degrees as the freezing point. We now use Celsius's scale, but the other way round: freezing point is at zero degrees and boiling point is at 100 degrees.

So Celsius's scale really measured cold, not heat!

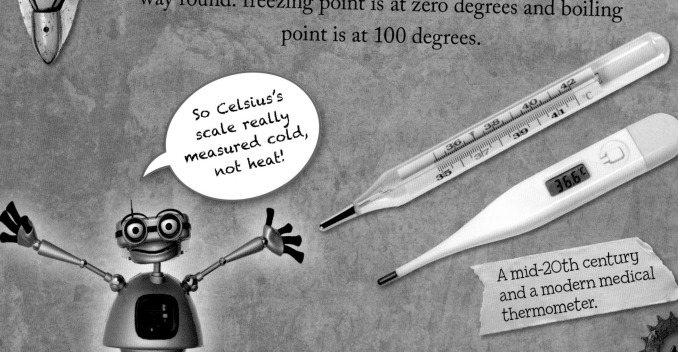

A mid-20th century and a modern medical thermometer.

Pay up!

Imagine if people had to pay for a car or a house or a holiday with just coins – they would need to push it about in wheelbarrows!

Easier to move around than a wheelbarrow full of coins is a promise to give someone a wheelbarrow full of coins if they ask for it. This is called a "promissary note", and these notes first appeared in China around 1400 years ago. People began trading promissory notes as if they were money. In 1024, the authorities in China started printing and issuing the notes and they actually became **paper money**.

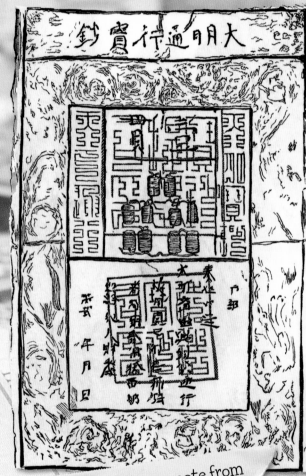

A Chinese promissory note from about 500 years ago.

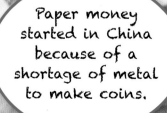

Paper money started in China because of a shortage of metal to make coins.

An early Swedish banknote

Nearly 600 years later, in 1661, the Stockholms Banco in Sweden was the first to issue **banknotes**, bringing paper money to Europe.

Before

Long before paper money was used by living people, it was used by the dead! At Chinese funerals, it was burned on a pyre along with the dead person to pay their fare to the afterlife.

With paper money, you still have to carry the money with you. **Credit cards** let you shop using a plastic card, and pay later. Now, credit cards can be used to buy meals, clothes, treats – almost anything. But the very first credit card could only be used to buy airline tickets. The **Air Travel Card**, issued in 1934, could be used with any of 17 airlines. The first credit card accepted as a method of payment by a range of businesses was the Diner's Club card, introduced in 1950.

An American credit card from the 1950s.

Striking a light

Imagine how difficult it would be to light a fire without matches. We don't use them very often today – perhaps just for lighting birthday cake candles. But before central heating and electric or gas cookers, fire was a part of everyday life.

The first, self-igniting **match** was made by Jean Chancel in France, in 1805. It had to be dipped into sulphuric acid, which is a very dangerous liquid, so the matches were not very practical – or safe – to use. Then in 1826, Englishman John Walker invented the first friction matches that could be lit by striking. Each match had to be drawn through a folded piece of sandpaper, which risked setting fire to the paper. They were soon banned in France and Germany.

Before

Before matches, people often carried a tinder box. It held a flint, which was struck against steel to make a spark, and "tinder" – material that caught light easily, such as dry moss.

The next version of the match used white phosphorous on its tip. It's so poisonous that each packet of matches contained enough phosphorous to kill an adult. The people who made the matches often developed a terrible condition called "phossy jaw", which caused their jaw bones to rot away.

Don't play with matches – even safety matches aren't that safe!

Red phosphorous is less dangerous than white phosphorus, and soon replaced it as the ignition agent (a substance that catches fire easily) on the top of each match. Matches only became reliable when the chemicals that produced the flame were separated, meaning that one chemical was put on the match head and the other put on to the side of the box – just like the matches and matchboxes you see today.

Going with a bang

Gunpowder is made of tiny grains of mixed chemicals that react together. But those little particles are capable of creating a lot of light and noise!

Gunpowder is an explosive chemical mixture of sulphur, charcoal, and potassium nitrate. It produces a huge amount of energy and gas when it burns. Burning gunpowder can be used to push something forwards, as the gas streams out behind.

Gunpowder was first discovered in the ninth century, by Chinese **alchemists** (ancient scientists). It was used in fireworks and the first cannons and guns. Use of gunpowder slowly spread westwards, reaching Europe in the 1200s.

Early Chinese fireworks.

Dynamite is an explosive mixture based on the chemical nitroglycerin mixed into something absorbent, such as a sawdust. It was invented by the Swedish chemist **Alfred Nobel** in 1867. He was looking for a powerful explosive to help blast away rocks and stone in excavation and mining. Using dynamite, it's possible to blow apart cliff faces in seconds.

Dynamite in action.

In 1888, newspapers printed a mistaken announcement of Nobel's death. One account wrote that he had "become rich by finding ways to kill more people faster than ever before". Upset by this, he set up the **Nobel Prizes** for outstanding work for peace and in science and literature. The peace prize was later won by famous names such as Nelson Mandela and Malala Yousafzai.

We need metal from mines to make lots of technologies, including robots!

We live in a technological age – you probably use technology nearly every minute of the day.

Clockwork

Long ago, people measured time using falling sand or water, or with sundials.

The first clock towers had clocks driven by falling water. Then around 1300, town clocks in Europe began to use an early type of clockwork mechanism driven by weights and a coiled rope. A set of **gears** moved two metal plates on a rod. They would alternately "tick" and "tock" as they engaged in turn with a saw-toothed wheel and moved the clock hand. These clocks had only an hour hand.

The oldest clock still working is at Salisbury Cathedral, UK. It dates from the 14th century.

A clock in Prague that shows astronomical information too.'

How it works

A clockwork mechanism has to be wound up. When you wind it, a spring inside the mechanism is tightly coiled. This stores potential energy – energy that can later be released as movement. As the spring uncoils, it drives gears that move the hands of the clock.

A clock needs a regular, repeated motion that always takes the same amount of time to complete, and a way of counting the movements. From the fifteenth century, some clocks used coiled metal springs. Two hundred years later, they could be made small enough to carry around as pocket watches. The big breakthrough came in 1675 when the Dutch scientist Christiaan Huygens added a **pendulum**. This regulated the clock even as it wound down, making it much more accurate. A minute hand and then a second hand were added.

After

The latest clocks are atomic, with the vibrations of a caesium **atom** providing the time-keeping. The atom vibrates 9,192,631,770 times a second. The best **atomic** clocks are accurate to a millionth of a second every year!

Picture perfect

We think nothing of taking a digital photo now. It's stored as an electronic image on a memory card. Originally, photographs were produced chemically.

Nicéphore Niépce was a patient man. It probably took several days to take the first photographs using his process of **heliography** in 1822. He covered a sheet of glass, stone or metal with bitumen (a tarry substance) dissolved in oil, and focussed an image onto it. Over a long time, the bitumen in the light hardened and he dissolved away the other parts to leave an image.

The first ever photo: View from the Window at Le Gras, 1826/7.

Louis Daguerre developed a better, quicker technique in 1839, called **daguerreotype**. Light fell onto a flat sheet of metal or glass (called a plate) with a coating of the compound silver iodide. Light changed the chemicals to produce an image in a few minutes. The process used large heavy plates, one for each image. The image was printed from the plate or film to make a permanent picture.

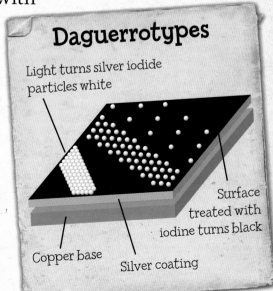

Daguerrotypes

Light turns silver iodide particles white

Surface treated with iodine turns black

Copper base

Silver coating

An early colour photo by Sergey Mikhaylovich Prokudin-Gorsky.

A positive image is the image we usually see. A negative image has dark and light areas reversed.

From then to now

1816: Nicéphore Niépce produces negative images, but they quickly disappear when exposed to light

1822: Niépce makes the first permanent photographic images, using his technique of heliography

1839: Louis Daguerre produces the daguerreotype and photography takes off

1861: The first colour photograph is demonstrated, but the method is not practical

1884: George Eastman makes the first photographic film

1888: The first Kodak camera is produced

1901: The Kodak Brownie makes photography affordable for many people

1935: The first good-quality colour film, from Kodak

1990s: Digital cameras appear and start to replace film camera.

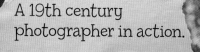

A 19th century photographer in action.

Power hungry

You probably use things powered by electricity all day long. It can be delivered through the mains or in forms such as batteries and photovoltaic cells.

Frogs played a part in the development of the first **battery**. The Italian biologist **Luigi Galvani** found that if he put a frog leg between two pieces of metal of different types, electricity could flow through the set-up. In 1800, Alessandro Volta swapped the frog legs for cardboard soaked in salt-water, and made the first battery from a sandwich of slices of zinc and copper with soggy cardboard squashed in between. We don't know what he did with the electricity he made.

Volta demonstrating his early battery.

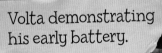

Zinc and copper sandwiches? Sounds like my lunch!

A modern power station can be the size of a small town!

Nuclear power comes from smashing atoms. Atoms are incredibly tiny, but the energy released is huge. A **neutron** is used to split an atom, releasing energy, and more neutrons, which then go on to split more atoms. This is known as a chain reaction. The Hungarian-American physicist Leó Szilárd first worked out how to start a nuclear chain reaction in 1933. The first application of a chain reaction was in an atomic bomb in 1945. The first nuclear power station was built in 1954 in Obninsk, Russia.

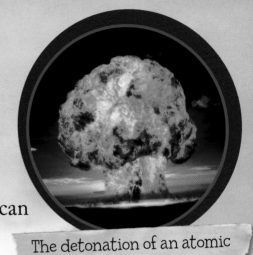

The detonation of an atomic bomb creates a huge mushroom cloud.

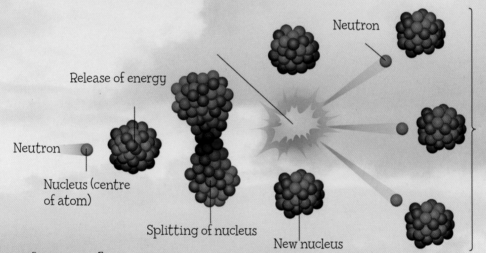

Release of energy

Neutron

Nucleus (centre of atom)

Splitting of nucleus

New nucleus

Neutron

Chain reaction

A **photovoltaic cell** collects energy from sunlight and turns it into electricity. Nineteen-year-old Edmond Becquerel made the first photovoltaic cell in his father's laboratory in France in 1839. Experimental cells appeared in the 19th century, but the first useful solar cells were made by Bell Laboratories in 1954. They were used to power satellites.

Computers

Computers are all around us, in our phones, cameras, cars and so many of the devices we use on a daily basis. Yet only 50 years ago, no one had their own computer.

Charles Babbage designed the first programmable computers in the 1820s. He called them his **Difference Engine** and Analytical Engine. They were entirely mechanical, using no electricity. The first computer programmer was Ada Lovelace, who developed programs for Babbage's Engines that were read from punched cards. The Engines were designed to work out calculations needed to make charts for shipping.

Part of Colossus, Mark 2, 1944

The first electronic computer was Colossus, designed by Tommy Flowers. It was built in secret at Bletchley Park, England, in 1944 to crack the codes the German army was using to send messages during World War II. Ten of the computers, each the size of a room, were made, and all were destroyed after the war. Programs were created by making physical wiring connections, which had to be changed for each new program.

Ferranti Mark 1

From then to now

1623: Wilhelm Schickard made a mechanical "Calculating Clock" that could add and subtract 6-digit numbers

1642: Blaise Pascal devised a mechanical adding machine

1801: Joseph-Marie Jacquard made an automated loom (for weaving), controlled by punched cards

1822: Charles Babbage completed his first design for a Difference Engine

1944: Colossus, first electronic programmable computer, built

1946: First general-purpose electronic programmable computer, ENIAC, USA

1948: First computer that could store programs – "Baby", UK

1951: First commercial computer – Ferranti Mark 1, developed from Baby

1975: First personal computer – Altair 8800, USA, sold as a kit. It had no screen, keyboard, mouse, or disk storage

1981: First IBM PC, USA

1983: First personal computer to use a desktop interface – Apple Lisa, USA.

My ancestors!

Apple Lisa

WWW.when?

The Internet and the World Wide Web are not the same thing. The Internet is a vast network of computers that spans the globe, and even has a few outposts in space. The World Wide Web is a set of web "pages" stored on some of those linked computers.

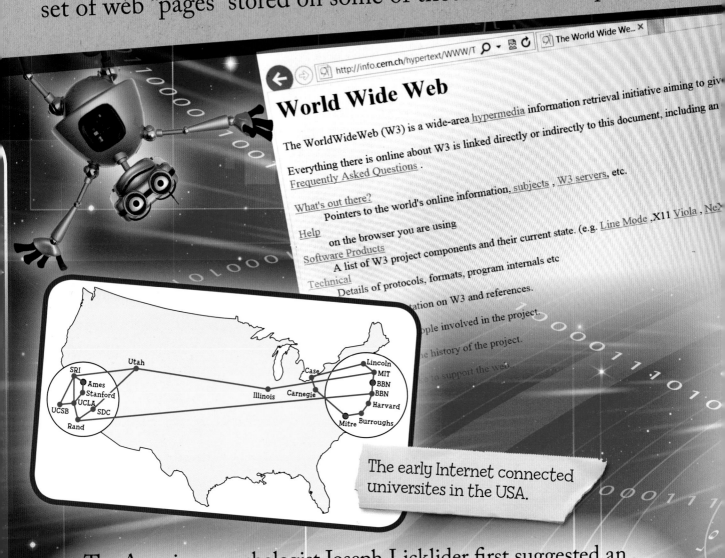

http://info.cern.ch/hypertext/WWW/T

The World Wide We... ×

World Wide Web

The WorldWideWeb (W3) is a wide-area hypermedia information retrieval initiative aiming to give

Everything there is online about W3 is linked directly or indirectly to this document, including an
Frequently Asked Questions .

What's out there?
    Pointers to the world's online information, subjects , W3 servers, etc.
Help
    on the browser you are using
Software Products
    A list of W3 project components and their current state. (e.g. Line Mode ,X11 Viola , NeX
Technical
    Details of protocols, formats, program internals etc

ation on W3 and references.

ple involved in the project.

he history of the project.

to support the web.

The early Internet connected universites in the USA.

The American psychologist Joseph Licklider first suggested an **intergalactic computer network** that would allow everyone to share and store information of all types. The first bit of Internet was developed by joining computers on four university sites in 1969 (three in California, one in Utah). It was called **ARPANET**. Other networks joined onto it to make a network of networks, which is why it is called the **Internet** – an inter-network network.

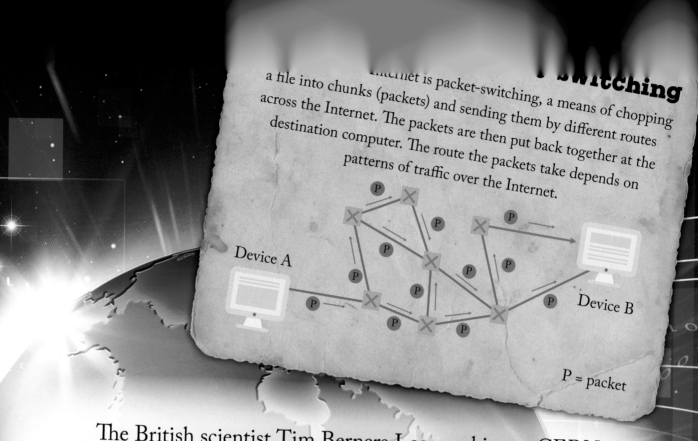

...Internet is packet-switching, a means of chopping a file into chunks (packets) and sending them by different routes across the Internet. The packets are then put back together at the destination computer. The route the packets take depends on patterns of traffic over the Internet.

Device A

Device B

P = packet

The British scientist Tim Berners Lee, working at CERN in Switzerland, wanted a way to share files with other people working on similar tasks. He brought **hypertext** and the Internet together, designing **HTML** as the language for writing web pages. In 1991, when the web started, it showed only text. But in 1993, the new Mosaic web browser added pictures and it took off. Web pages are still written in later versions of HTML.

Printing in solids

Y ou might have a printer you use with your computer to print documents – two-dimensional objects. But how about a printer that can make three-dimensional objects?

American engineer **Chuck Hall** developed the first **3-D printer** in 1984. He called the process **stereolithography**, but it's also called additive manufacturing (AM). At first, 3-D printing was used only for making prototypes – early working models of a device. 3-D printing works by following a pattern to lay down layers of plastic or metal, which hardens into a shape that has been designed and defined on a computer. To build up an object, the computer sends the information for one thin slice after another to the printer.

From the 2000s, 3-D printing has developed into mass production. It is now used with all types of engineering. It can be used to make engine parts, medical appliances, and even fashion items.

It's a cheap and easy way to make exact replicas of parts needed for one-off items, such as very old aircraft. To do this, the object is either designed on computer, or it's scanned with a **3-D scanner** to make a complete model of it on a computer. Then the information is cut into lots of cross-sections of the object, which the printer can understand.

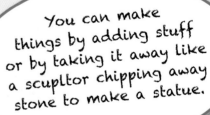

You can make things by adding stuff or by taking it away like a scupltor chipping away stone to make a statue.

CHAPTER 6: SIGHT AND SOUND

How often do you use something other than just your eyes to see things? There are very big and very small things we can't see well – or at all – with the naked eye.

I spy

If you don't have very good eyesight, you can easily get spectacles or contact lenses. But it hasn't always been so easy.

Eye-glasses to correct sight were first used in Italy around 1286. They began as two separate lenses placed over the eyes, but soon someone thought to join them with a nose-piece, making it easier to keep them in place. The Italian monk, Savonarola, suggested adding a ribbon to tie them on.

The first lenses were **convex** (rounded outwards) and could correct only far-sightedness (when people can only focus on objects far away). Most people develop far-sightedness as they age, and these early corrective glasses were useful for them.

Before

The Romans discovered that small objects could appear magnified by looking at them through a glass globe filled with water or a curved lens.

No one knew why eye-glasses worked until 1604. Then, the German astronomer Johannes Kepler explained how convex and **concave** lenses change the point where light is focussed. The right lenses can correct far-sightedness and short-sightedness (when people can only focus on objects nearby).

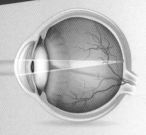
NORMAL VISION
Near object is clear.

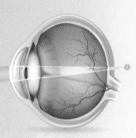
FARSIGHTED EYE
The eyeball
is too short.
Near object is blurry.

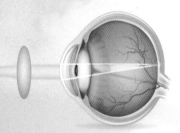
FARSIGHTEDNESS
CORRECTED
Correction
with a lens

Sunglasses were invented in China in the 12th century. They were made of smoky quartz, a see-through crystal with a grey tinge. The Inuit had used walrus-bone goggles with a slit in the front to protect their eyes from the sun since prehistoric times.

Early sunglasses.

Seeing small

Most living things on the planet are microorganisms – life-forms too small to see with the naked eye. Until the 1600s, no one knew they existed.

The **microscope** was invented in the Netherlands in the 1590s, but we don't know who by.

A

B

C

D

Leeuwenhoek's microscope, from around 1600. The sample is held on a pin (B), moved into position and focus using the screws C and D, and viewed from the lens (A).

Later microscopes held lenses at fixed distances in tubes, adding more and better lenses to achieve greater magnification. These microscopes all reflect and magnify light falling on the object. They are called **optical microscopes**. From the mid-1600s, scientists began to use microscopes to examine living things and tissues.

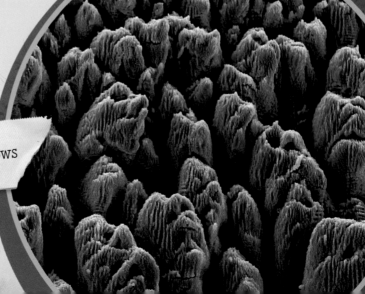

The surface of silicon seen through a microscope shows riippled microstructures

One of the most important scientists was **Antonie van Leeuwenhoek**, who discovered red blood cells and, in 1676, found and described **microorganisms**. The discovery revolutionized science – suddenly, it was clear that the world was teeming with life. Even substances that looked entirely lifeless like water and mud were packed with tiny organisms. Looking at the human body through the microscope helped scientists begin to understand how the body works.

A virus seen through a powerful microscope.

The most powerful modern microscopes use beams of electrons rather than light to produce images of the specimen. The first electron microscope was made by Ernst Ruska and Max Knoll in 1931. The best electron microscopes can show a specimen at 10,000,000 x its real size. The best optical microscopes produce magnification less than 2,000 x.

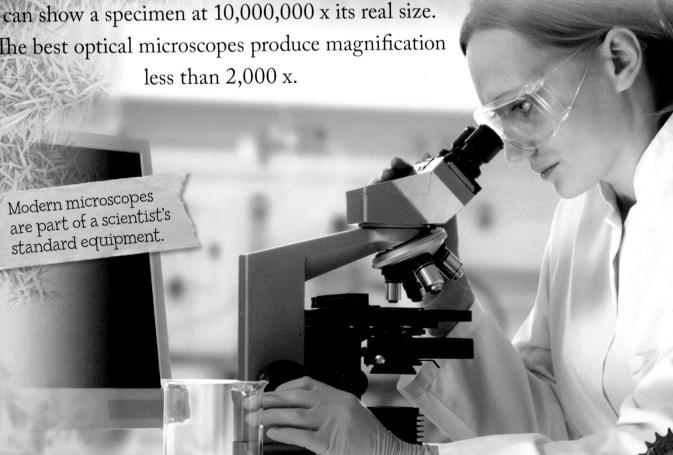

Modern microscopes are part of a scientist's standard equipment.

Gazing into the distance

If you look up at the night sky, everything except the moon is just a point of light. But if you look through a telescope, you can see the planets more clearly and can see many more stars.

The **optical telescope** was invented in the Netherlands in 1608, by Hans Lippershey, Zacharias Janssen, and Jacob Metius. Galileo heard of the invention in 1609 and built his own within a month. He went on to make a much better one the following year. Galileo used his telescope to look at the planets and discovered that they are other worlds, some with their own moons. This revolutionized humanity's view of the universe, showing that our world is not the only one.

Galileo demonstrates his telescope.

Telescopes could scan the horizon from ships, too.

Optical telescopes use a system of lenses and mirrors to magnify faraway objects. The larger the lens, the larger the magnification possible. The first radio telescope was built by Grote Reber in 1937. **Radio telescopes** work by picking up radio waves, and then making a visible image from the information collected.

The dish of a radio telescope focusses the radio waves onto the end of the antenna in the centre, which then reflects them all to a receiver on the edge of the dish. The collected data is then sent to be processed by a computer to generate an image.

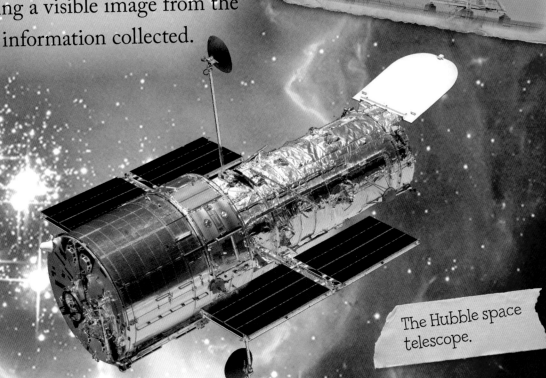

The Hubble space telescope.

Optical telescopes suffer from interference from Earth's atmosphere and from light pollution. To avoid these problems, some telescopes are sited in space. The first space-based optical telescope was **Hipparcos**, launched in 1989 by the European Space Agency. The famous **Hubble Space Telescope** was launched about six months later, in 1990.

Sounds good

We take recorded music for granted. But until recently, the only way to hear something was to listen to it live.

The first sound recording was made by Édouard-Léon Scott de Martinville in France in 1857, using a needle to scratch a track onto paper coated with soot. His recordings could not be played back, though.

Mechanical recording

Sound is carried as vibrations through air, water or solids. Mechanical recording methods use the vibrations to move a needle over a surface (such as a wax cylinder), recording a track. The wiggly line produced on a wax cylinder or record can be converted back from movements of a needle to sound and replayed.

Thomas Edison was the first person to record and play back sound, in 1877. He used a needle to record a trace onto a cylinder covered in tin foil. The foil was fragile, so soon cylinders were made of wax. They could be mass-produced – everyone could buy a **phonograph** and a collection of recorded music. But the wax cylinders wore out, so frrom 1900 cylinders were made of a hard, early plastic that lasted better.

Edison's phonograph.

In 1889, Emile Berliner sold an alternative – a **gramophone** that took disks rather than cylinders. In the 1920s, gramophones took over from phonographs.

The first records were made from shellac – a brittle material produced as resin by lac insects.

From then to now

1920s: First reel-to-reel tape recorders, using steel tape

1963: Audio cassette tapes let everyone make recordings

1982: Audio CD introduced by Sony and Philips

1991: MPEG-1 becomes the standard format for digital sound files.

An early gramophone.

CHAPTER 7: MATERIALS

Everything is made of something, and while some materials – like wood and clay – are used as they are found, others need some kind of processing or manufacture to be usable.

An ancient Chinese spinning wheel.

Spinning a yarn

Wool comes from sheep (or other animals) – but we can't use it straightaway. It must first be spun into yarn to be used for knitting or weaving.

The **spinning wheel** was the first mechanical means of making thread. It was invented in China, around 1,000 AD, to spin silk. European travellers took the technology home in the 1100s, and spinning wheels were used there to spin wool and flax (the plant fibre used to make linen). A spinning wheel draws out a thread from a clump of wool and winds it on a **bobbin** or **spindle**. The first wheels were turned by hand.

Before

For centuries, people spun wool using a distaff and spindle. The raw wool is packed onto the distaff, then the spinner pulls out a fibre and winds it around the spindle. By constantly pulling and winding, they spin a thread around the spindle.

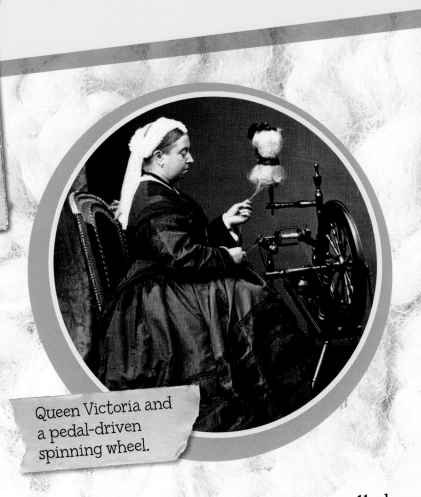

Queen Victoria and a pedal-driven spinning wheel.

A medieval woman uses a distaff to spin wool.

Later spinning wheels were controlled by a foot pedal, or turned by the power of water.

In 1764, the Englishman James Hargreaves combined several spindles with one wheel, setting them in a frame. He called it the **Spinning Jenny.** It meant one worker could produce a great deal of yarn very easily. He began with eight spindles and increased their number to 120.

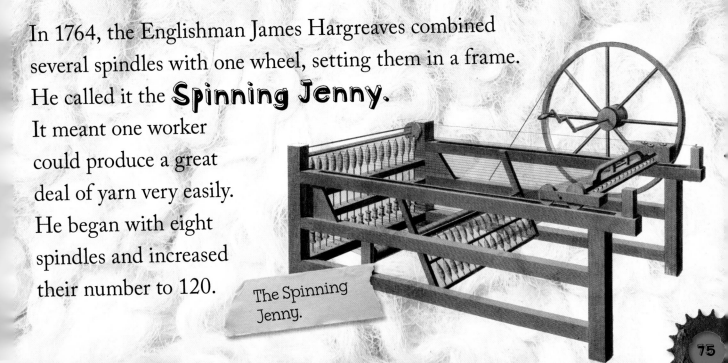

The Spinning Jenny.

Cotton pickin'

Cotton grows on shrubs as a protective "boll" (like a blob) of fibres around the seeds of the cotton plant. The biggest problem for cotton workers has always been to separate the cotton fibres from the seeds.

Simple rollers and a flat stone were used for removing seeds from cotton from the 5th century BC, but they often crushed the seeds and mashed them into the fibres. Some time before 1313 in China, **a double-roller system** appeared. It had two rollers fitted close together in a wooden frame, turning in opposite directions. The cotton was forced between the rollers, which squeezed out the seeds as the cotton fibre went through.

Whitney's cotton gin.

In 1793, American Eli Whitney invented the **cotton gin**, a mechanical device with a wire grille, rather like a comb, over a wooden cylinder fitted with tiny hooks. As the handle was turned, the hooks caught on the cotton fibres and pulled them through the mesh. The seeds were too large to fit through and were left behind. It's said that Whitney came up with his design after watching a cat claw at a chicken through a wire fence and managing to hook only feathers.

Whitney's invention made cotton farming much more profitable. Sadly, this led to the expansion of cotton plantations in America, and an increase in **slavery**. The number of slaves rose from 700,000 in 1790 to around 3.2 million in 1850.

A large-scale cotton gin.

Some people say the cotton gin led indirectly to the American Civil War of 1861-1865. Machines always get the blame!

New materials

Cotton, wool and silk are all naturally occurring materials, but some materials have been invented – they are synthetic, or man-made.

There are lots of different types of **plastic** now. The very first was called Parkesine, invented by Alexander Parkes in the UK in 1856. It was made from plant material (cellulose) treated with nitric acid, and was often used as fake ivory. It was the hard, brittle **Bakelite** invented by Leo Baekeland in the USA in 1907 that really began the age of plastics. It was used in casings for electrical items and kitchen utensils amongst other items.

A Bakelite radio.

Polystyrene was created accidentally in 1839, and made deliberately from 1931. Expanded **polystyrene** is used for packing materials and insulated cups for hot drinks. **PVC** was also discovered accidentally and ignored before being made commercially in 1926. It can be rigid – as in drainpipes – or flexible, as in raincoats.

Nylon was invented by Wallace Carothers in the USA in 1935 as a replacement for silk. Nylon was first used for toothbrushes (in 1938) and then for women's stockings (1940). During World War II it was used instead of silk for parachutes. Nylon can be a solid plastic or a fibre.

A toothbrush advert from the 1950s.

Toothbrush bristles are still made from Nylon.

Super-strong **Kevlar** was developed to be stronger than steel. It's used for boats, tyres, body armour, cables and many other items. It was discovered accidentally by the Polish-American chemist Stephanie Kwolek in 1964 while she was looking for a new material for making tyres.

A modern boat made from Kevlar.

CHAPTER 8: AT HOME

Imagine how nasty it would be if you didn't have a flush toilet. Lots of very old civilizations made basic toilets, but we didn't get it right until the 1500s.

Flush it away

The easiest way to get rid of waste is to dump it in a hole – but that's rather smelly. Flushing is better!

Sir John Harrington was sent away from Queen Elizabeth I's court in 1584 for telling rude jokes. So he built himself a new house, and installed a **flushing toilet** of his own design. Turning a handle tipped water into the toilet, opening a leather valve at the bottom and washing the waste into a cess pool (which had to be emptied by servants). He called his toilet **Ajax**, and later made one for the queen.

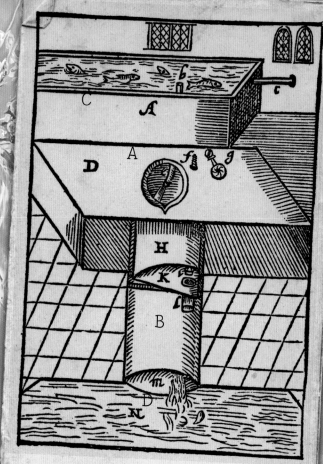

Harrington's toilet has a circular seat (A), leading to a waste pipe (B) below that empties into a pool. Fresh water comes from a cistern above (C) - with fish!

Before

Many older civilizations had early types of toilet flushed clean by water. The oldest might have been in Neolithic Britain 5,000 years ago. The Indus Valley civilisation, north of India, had many homes with a type of flush toilets 3,000 years ago.

The **S-trap** is a pipe with an S-shaped bend that traps water in the middle of the "S". It was invented in 1775 by Alexander Cumming. The waste is flushed past the S, but a final pool of water is left in it, which stops nasty smells coming back up the toilet. This new design of toilet caught on, and when a large sewerage system was built in London in the nineteenth century, flush toilets became common.

A Victorian toilet.

Japanese toilets come with heated seats, adjustable washjets, hot air drying and music!

In Japan, there are robotic toilets!

Dinner time!

We take it for granted that we can buy food on Monday and eat it on Friday without being sick. But it hasn't always been easy to prevent food from rotting.

In the 1860s, the French biologist **Louis Pasteur** discovered that food goes bad because of the work of microbes (germs). He found that soup and milk last much longer if they are heated to kill the microbes – 'pasteurized' – and then covered to prevent more microbes getting in. Pasteurizing milk was first suggested by Franz von Soxhlet in Germany in 1886. Most milk is now pasteurized.

A modern pasteurization facility.

Canned food first appeared in the Netherlands in the mid-1700s. By 1772, the Dutch navy was taking **canned food** on long sea voyages. The food – such as roast beef – was cooked, put into a metal canister, and covered with hot fat. The can was sealed by soldering on a lid. People used whatever tools they had to open a can. Life became a lot easier when the can opener was invented in the 1850s.

Cans from the early 1900s.

People in very cold climates have long preserved food by natural freezing. The first refrigeration system was invented by Jacob Perkins in 1834. It used the cooling effect of gas compressed into a liquid and then evaporating. In 1929, Clarence Birdseye invented **flash-freezing** after seeing frozen food in Labrador, Canada.

In 1626, the English scientist Francis Bacon experimented with **freezing food**, stuffing snow into and around a dead chicken. Sadly, he developed bronchitis and died. The ghost of the chicken is said to haunt Pond Square in London.

Frrrrridge

These days you don't have to flash-freeze food then go to the bother of defrosting it before you eat it. You can simply put it in the **fridge**, and it will stay fresh for much longer than if you leave out in the air.

Early fridges had a large cooling unit on top.

A Scottish inventor made a small refrigeration system in 1755, but it took until 1834 for a Jacob Perkins to invent a practical refrigerator. It used the cooling effect of gas compressed into a liquid and then evaporating.

How it works

Evaporation refrigeration uses a liquid with a very low boiling point (the refrigerant) which circulates in a loop of pipes inside and outside the fridge.

1. The refrigerant gas is sucked from inside the fridge and compressed into a warm liquid
2. Heat escapes from the warm liquid outside the fridge
3. The refrigerant is forced through a narrow gap just before it goes back into the fridge and expands to become a cold gas
4. The cold gas absorbs heat from inside the fridge

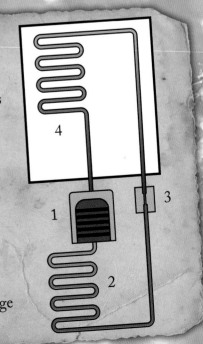

Before

The icebox was once a common household item in the USA. A box with insulated walls held a large block of ice that melted slowly, cooling food. The block had to be replaced frequently, with ice brought down from the mountains.

Iceboxes filled with warm water if you didn't change the ice often enough!

A Model A-562 refrigerator from 1930.

Other inventors found different ways of using the action of evaporation to create a cooling effect, but the first to catch on and become a product was invented by two Swedish students, Baltzar von Platen and Carl Munters, in 1922. Their fridge went into commercial production in 1925 and was incredibly successful. The company that made it was bought up by Electrolux in 1925.

A **freezer** is really just a super-duper fridge. It works in the same way, but with a greater cooling effect to keep the contents below the freezing point of water.

A stitch in time...

We all wear clothes, and someone has to make them. For thousands of years people stitched clothes by hand. It was slow, so clothes cost a lot and most people had very few.

Then in France, in 1829, Barthelemy Thimonnier had a better idea. Like most other **tailors**, Thimonnier was poor. He made friends with Auguste Ferrand, an engineer, and they developed a **sewing machine** made of wood and metal. It worked slightly faster than sewing by hand. In 1830, Thimonnier opened a factory, making uniforms for the French army. Local tailors, worried that his invention was stealing their work, stormed the factory and burned all his machines.

A replica of a Thimonnier sewing machine.

While Thimonnier wanted to use the sewing machine to earn money from making clothes, the American Elias Howe designed a sewing machine to sell. In 1845, his machine introduced the **lockstitch** method that is still used. One thread is carried through the fabric by a needle with an eye near the point, and another thread running underneath the fabric locks it in place.

Isaac Singer soon started making and selling similar machines, but these were driven by a foot treadle. Singer set up the first hire purchase scheme so that people could buy a sewing machine, paying for it slowly over time.

A sewing machine driven by a foot treadle.

Howe and Singer argued over patents and Howe won. Singer had to pay him $1.15 for each sewing machine he sold. Howe made enough money to fund his own Unionist regiment in the American Civil War. He served in his regiment as a private.

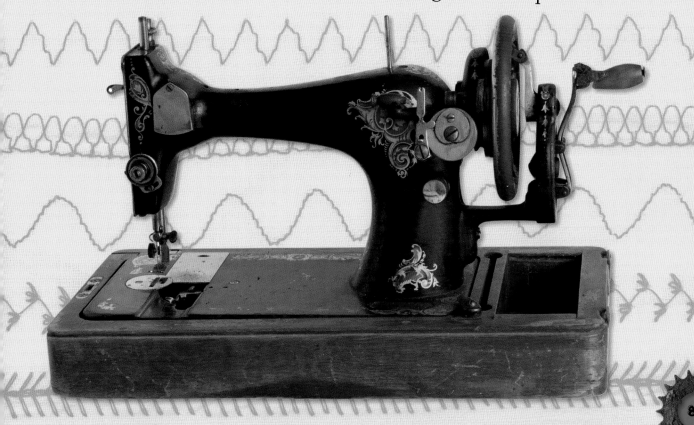

Lights on!

Imagine what it would be like if you couldn't turn the lights on at night. That's how it used to be.

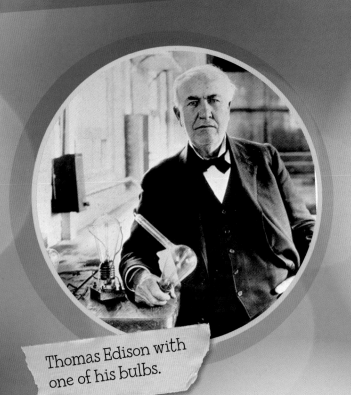

Thomas Edison with one of his bulbs.

The first building lit by **electric light** was Joseph Swan's house in England, in 1878. One of the inventors of the **light bulb**, Swan installed lights in his own home first. Swan, and Thomas Edison (in the USA), were the first people to make a practical light bulb. But they were not the first to think of it.

The English chemist Humphry Davy showed in 1802 that passing current from an early battery through a strip of platinum produced a bright glow. For the next 75 years, chemists experimented using bulbs containing different gases or a vacuum, looking for a metal that would glow without melting.

Before

For thousands of years, people used candles and oil lamps, but both are dangerous, smelly and smoky. Then William Murdoch invented gas lighting, burning coal gas to produce light, and lit his own home in England with gas from 1792. Gas lighting became common in homes and for street lighting.

In 1835, Scotsman James Lindsay made a bulb he could read by. Having done that, he didn't develop it further or try to sell it, but moved on to new projects. It was left for Swan and Edison to perfect the bulb. Both settled on a **carbon filament** (the curly wire inside a bulb) in a vacuum. After Edison's bulbs were successfully installed on a steamship they were adopted for wider use.

Before fairy lights, Christmas trees were decorated with candles.

The light bulb has become a symbol of briliant ideas!

What's left to invent?

It's tempting to think all the good things have been invented already – but there's always scope for something new. Some inventions are very complicated and lots of people work on them together.

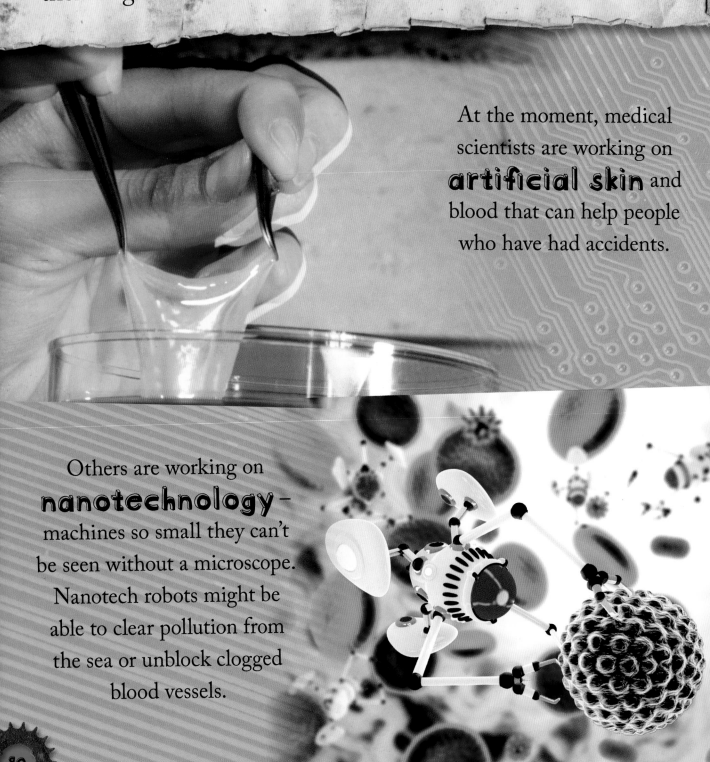

At the moment, medical scientists are working on **artificial skin** and blood that can help people who have had accidents.

Others are working on **nanotechnology** – machines so small they can't be seen without a microscope. Nanotech robots might be able to clear pollution from the sea or unblock clogged blood vessels.

Not all inventions are complicated. Some are just very good, simple ideas. In 2014, 15-year-old **Ann Makosinski** invented a torch that works from the heat of the hand holding it, and it doesn't need any other power source. And 18-year-old **Eesha Khare** invented a mobile phone charger that fully charges a phone in 20-30 seconds.

Ann Makosinski demonstrates her torch.

Eesha Khare talks about her invention.

Perhaps you could be the next great inventor. It takes **ingenuity**, creativity and determination. You might need some scientific or mechanical knowledge – but the most important thing is a new way of looking at the world and its problems.

Which new invention would you most like to see? Don't sit around waiting for someone else to invent it – get thinking!

Every invention starts with an idea, but it's only an invention if it's actually made and it works!

Glossary

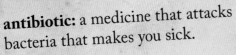

antibiotic: a medicine that attacks bacteria that makes you sick.

anaesthetic: a chemical used to prevent you feeling pain; it can send you to sleep, or numb part of your body.

antibody: part of the body's response to fight disease.

atom: a tiny particle that everything in the world is made up of; the smallest type of particle that makes up matter of all types.

bacteria: tiny living thing (microorganism); some bacteria cause diseases.

barometer: an instrument for measuring air pressure.

bobbin: a cylinder around which wire or thread is wound.

brake block: the block that presses against the wheels of a vehicle to make it stop.

brake lining: the tough, replaceable surface of a brake.

caesium: a soft, silvery-gold metal.

concave: curved inwards.

convex: curved outwards.

cordage: rope.

diesel: a fuel that burns without a spark but only when put under great pressure.

DNA: complex chemical that carries a code recording the genetic (inherited) information about an organism (for example a plant or animal).

electromagnetic radiation: waves of energy, including light, radio, X-rays and microwaves.

electron: small "packet" of electrical charge.

embryo: an unborn child or animal in the early stages of development.

evaporate: to change state from liquid to gas.

gears: toothed wheels that lock together to transmit motion, often used to change the speed or direction of motion in a machine.

gene: a string of DNA that holds the code for specific inherited features of an organism (such as a plant or animal).

hypertext: a system for displaying linked information including text, images, sound and video; the World Wide Web uses hypertext .

ingenuity: cleverness in discovering, planning or inventing.

insulated: protected against the effects of electricity or heat.

integrated circuit board: a set of electronic circuits printed onto a single board. They are used in computers, mobile phones and other electronic equipment.

locomotive: a self-propelled vehicle used to pull carriages or trailers.

navigate: to direct the course of a ship or aircraft.

neutron: a particle in the nucleus (middle) of an atom. Unlike other subatomic particles, it has no electrical charge.

nutrient: a chemical component of food that people, animals and plants need in order to survive.

patent: a legal document recording that someone owns the design of an invention, and which prevents other people copying and selling it without permission.

pendulum: a weight hung from a fixed point so that it can swing freely.

pharmaceutical: relating to the manufacture of medicines.

piston: a mechanical device used in engines that plunges backwards and forwards inside a hollow cylinder.

satellite: a human-made or natural object that is in orbit around a planet or moon.

silicon chip: a very small piece of the metal silicon on which electronic circuits are etched (drawn on with acid).

sterilize: to destroy germs through heat or the action of chemicals.

taffeta: a crisp, smooth material made from either silk or man-made fibre.

tailor: a person who makes or repairs clothing.

telegraph: a device used to send coded messages over long distances using electricity.

transistor: a small electronic device used in a circuit as a switch.

vaccine: a sample of a weakened or changed disease that is given to a healthy person to help protect them against catching the disease in its full form.

vacuum: a space completely empty of matter, even air.

virus: a tiny scrap of DNA (or RNA, a similar chemical) that is on the border between living and not-living things. Some viruses can cause diseases.

wavelength: the distance between two peaks in a set of waves.

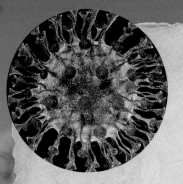

Index

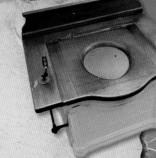

3-D printers 64–65

3-D scanners 65

adding machines 61

aircraft 7, 18–19

anaesthetics 8, 24–25, 26

Analytical Engine 60

antibiotics 9, 27

antibodies 23

antiseptics 26, 27

ARPANET 62

artificial skin and blood 90

atomic clocks 55

audio cassette tapes 73

Babbage, Charles 60, 61

Bacon, Francis 83

Baird, John Logie 42

Bakelite 78

ballpoint pens 33

banknotes 49

barbed wire 6

batteries 58

BBC 43

Becquerel, Edmond 59

Bell, Alexander Graham 38

Benz, Karl and Bertha 16

Berners Lee, Tim 63

bicycles 12–13

Birdseye, Clarence 83

biros 33

books 31

Braille 34

Braun, Wernher von 20–21

canned food 83

cars 8, 16–17

cathode ray tubes 42, 43

CDs 73

Celsius scale 47

Chain, Ernst 27

chain reactions 59

clocks 54–55, 61

Colossus 60

compasses 10–11

computers 6, 11, 60–61

cotton gins 76–77

credit cards 49

daguerreotypes 56, 57

Davy, Humphrey 88

Difference Engine 60, 61

dynamite 53

Edison, Thomas 72, 88, 89

electric motors 7

electricity 58, 59, 88–89

electromagnetic radiation 7, 40

electromagnets 37

electron microscopes 69

ether 24

eye-glasses 66–67

Fahrenheit scale 47

fairy lights 89

fireworks 52

flashlights 91

Fleming, Alexander 27

Florey, Howard 27

Flowers, Tommy 60

Ford, Henry 17

fountain pens 32

freezers 85

fridges 84–85

frozen food 83

Galileo Galilei 70

Galvani, Luigi 58

gas lighting 89

genetic engineering 28–29

glow-in-the-dark genes 29

Goddard, Robert 20

gramophones 73

gunpowder 8, 20, 52

Gutenberg, Johannes 31

Hall, Chuck 64

Hargreaves, James 75

Harrington, Sir John 80

heliography 56

Hertz, Heinrich 40

Hipparcos 71

hire purchase schemes 87

hot-air balloons 19

Howe, Elias 44, 86, 87

HTML 63

Hubble Space Telescope 71

Huygens, Christiaan 55

iceboxes 85

integrated circuit boards 7

internal combustion engines 17

Internet 41, 62–63

Jenner, Edward 23

jet engines 19, 21

Kevlar 79

Khare, Eesha 91

Kodak cameras 57

LED technology 43

Leeuwenhoek, Antonie van 69

light bulbs 88–89

Lindsay, James 89

Lister, Joseph 26

looms 61

Lovelace, Ada 60

Luddites 8

Maglev trains 15

Makosinski, Ann 91

Marconi, Guglielmo 40, 41

matches 50–51

Maxwell, James Clerk 40

microscopes 9, 68–69

mobile phone chargers 91

mobile phones 7, 39, 40

Model T Ford 17

Montgolfier brothers 19

Morse code 36, 40, 41

Morton, William 24

MPEG-1 73

Murdoch, William 89

nanotechnology 90

Newcomen, Thomas 14

Niépce, Nicéphore 56, 57

night writing 35

Nobel, Alfred 53

Nobel Prizes 53

nuclear power 59

nylon 79

packet-switching 63

paper money 48–49

Parkesine 78

pasteurization 82

patents 33, 44, 87

penicillin 27

phonographs 72

phosphorus 51

photography 56–57

photovoltaic cells 59

plastics 78

polystyrene 78

power stations 58, 59

printing 8, 9, 30–31

promissory notes 48

PVC 78

radar 40

radio 7, 40–41

radio telescopes 71

railroads 14, 15

refrigeration 83, 84–85

robots 21, 22, 27, 90

rockets 20–21

S-traps 81

SatNav 11

sewing machines 86–87

sign languages 35

silicon chips 7

Singer, Isaac 87

slavery 77

sound recordings 72–73

space exploration 20, 21, 45

Spinning Jenny 75

spinning wheels 74–75

steam engines 7, 14, 15

stereolithography 64

sunglasses 67

Swan, Joseph 88, 89

synthetic materials 78–79

Szilárd, Leó 59

tape recorders 73

telegraphy 8, 36, 37, 41

telephone exchanges 38, 39

telephones 38–39

telescopes 70–71

television 40, 42–43

thermometers 46–47

Thimonnier, Barthelemy 86

tinder boxes 50

toilets 80–81

trains 14–15

transistor radios 41

transistors 7

Trevithick, Richard 14

typewriters 33

tyres 16

V2 rockets 20, 21

vaccination 9, 22–23

Velcro 45

Volta, Alessandro 58

Watt, James 14

wheels 9, 11

Whitney, Elias 76

World Wide Web 9, 62, 63

Wright, Orville and Wilbur 18

zips 44

Picture Credits

Picture researcher: Jennifer Veall